I0176777

I Want to Pray!

Opening Communication with God

by

Perry M. Dalton

&

Henry E. Neufeld

(Revised and Expanded)

Energion Publications
P. O. Box 841
Gonzalez, FL 32560
http://www.energionpubs.com
pubs@energion.com

Energion Publications
P. O. Box 841
Gonzalez, FL 32560

Scripture quotations marked CEV are taken from the **Contemporary English Version**, Copyright © 1995 American Bible Society.

Scripture quotations marked NRSV are taken from the **New Revised Standard Version Bible**, copyright © 1989 by the Division of Christian Education of the National Council of the Churches of Christ in the U. S. A. Used by permission. All rights reserved.

Unmarked translations are by Henry E. Neufeld for this book. Henry's translations can be found on the Totally Free Bible Version page at http://hneufeld.com/tfbv.

Cover by Jason Neufeld, http://www.jasonneufelddesign.com

Copyright © 1998 & 2005, Henry E. Neufeld & Perry M. Dalton

ISBN: 1-893729-31-1

Table of Contents

1 - Prayer: Getting Personal with God

Do you believe that there is a God who just might answer prayers if you only knew how to talk to him? This book will discuss both how to talk and how to listen for those answers.

Do you wonder if there is a God out there, and want to try to get in touch? This book will help you discover the experience of prayer.

Did you grow up with prayer in church, but it never became part of your personal life? Let some of these simple approaches open up a personal prayer experience for you.

What if it has been a long time since you talked to God? What if you feel like he wouldn't want to listen to you? He *does* want to listen. Let these few simple suggestions get the conversation started.

How does this work?

The keys are experience and participation. That means that you must get involved personally in prayer, track your experiences, and let that experience show you the way. There are no formulas here, just a simple, conversational approach.

So why have a method at all? Many people find themselves tongue-tied when they are trying to talk to God. They may lose concentration when they try to listen to God. The trouble is that we have lost the childlike ability to talk to invisible friends. Now talking to invisible friends can be a problem. Not all invisible friends are there. Not all of them are *friendly*.

The idea of talking to invisible friends is sometimes used to make fun of prayer, but Jesus embraces the childlike nature required for His kingdom. Of children he says, "The kingdom of heaven is made up of that kind of people." (Matthew 19:14)

So this book is about talking to your one *invisible* friend. Or perhaps you could call it talking to your *spiritually visible* friend. As you experience the power of prayer in your life, the decision will be yours.

Chapter 1 Questions and Exercises

1. If you had a situation (good news or bad!) to whom would you go for wisdom or a listening ear? Where would you meet? What would make you most comfortable

Spouse

Pastor

Parent

Brother or Sister

Friend

Now think of the same scenario, but with God as your listener. It's OK for you to think of this as God the Father, Jesus, or the Holy Spirit.

Maybe you would go to a park or beach. Say what's on your mind to God. If you would just sit down together in the living room with the TV off and have a heart to heart talk, do that.

2. Do you have enough intimate times and conversations with people who are close to you in

your daily life? Discussion: If there is a need, how could you change?

3. Do you have enough intimate and personal times in your life with God? Discussion: If there is a need, how could you change?

4. Read Matthew 19:13-15. Do you want to approach God as a child? Why or why not? How could you do this?

Our LORD, you are true to your promises,
And your word is like silver
Heated seven times in a fiery furnace.

— Psalm 12:6

2 - The Most Basic Prayer

The most basic prayer is found in Luke 18:13 —
"The tax collector stood off at a distance and did not
think he was good enough even to look up toward
heaven. He was so sorry for what he had done that
he pounded his chest and prayed, 'God, have pity on
me! I am such a sinner.'"

Such a prayer need not be a prayer for forgiveness,
but it is simply a request for some one specific thing.
Starting to pray is just as simple as that. We will
study some more advanced prayers later in this
booklet, but once you have spoken a simple, one
sentence prayer, you are started on your prayer life.

Getting Started in Prayer

Here are some thoughts on getting started in prayer.

➢ Prayer does not need to be complex (Matthew
  6:7).
➢ You don't have to be good enough to pray (Luke
  18:9-14).
➢ Prayer can be private (Matthew 6:6).
➢ Prayer can be public (Acts 7:59, 60).

- ➢ Prayer can include both your needs and those of others (Matthew 6:9-13; James 1:5; 1 John 5:16).
- ➢ You can show love for one another in a group (1 John 4:7,20, Hebrews 10:25).

Examples of Prayer Scriptures

- ➢ General prayer (Matthew 6:9-13)
- ➢ Simple Petition (Luke 18:13)
- ➢ Healing (Acts 9:40, 41)
- ➢ Healing through Anointing (James 5:16)
- ➢ Pray and Work (Nehemiah 4:1-23; 5:1-19; 6:15-17)
- ➢ Confession and Repentance (Psalm 51)
- ➢ Wisdom (James 1:5-8)
- ➢ Blessing (Numbers 6:22-27)
- ➢ Worship (Psalm 84)
- ➢ Praise (2 Chronicles 20:22)

I encourage God's own people to have more faith and to understand the truth about religion. Then they will have the hope of eternal life that God promised long ago. And God never tells a lie!

— Titus 1:1,2

Chapter 2 Questions and Exercises

1. On what occasions might a very simple or short prayer be best?

The invocation at church
The pastoral prayer
Praying with someone who is ill
Praying with your child at bedtimes
Eating with someone in a restaurant
The blessing for your meal at home
A prayer for someone
A prayer of thanks or praise

2. Considering the same situations, when might your prayer be longer? How long should a prayer be?

"You should pray like this:

Our Father in heaven,
Help us to honor your name.
Come and set up your kingdom,
So that everyone on earth will obey you,
    as you are obeyed in heaven.
Give us our food for today.
Forgive us for doing wrong,
As we forgive others.
Keep us from being tempted
And protect us from evil."
– Matthew 6:9-13

3 - The General Prayer

When Jesus was asked how one should pray, he gave an approach to prayer that combines the following elements:

1. Acknowledgement of God as our parent and authority figure. We praise God and bring ourselves into subjection to his kingdom.
2. Asking for God's help in honoring Him. We admit our own limitations and ask for the power of God in our lives (Romans 1:16-17).
3. Inviting God's presence and His kingdom, not only in our hearts and lives, but also in the world at large.
4. Acknowledging God as the source of what we need and asking that he fulfill our needs. When we ask that our daily needs be supplied we place our trust continually in God's love and care.
5. Asking for forgiveness and determining to be forgiving.
6. Protection from testing and trial. When we ask for protection from testing and trial, we acknowledge that trial will come and we admit our own weakness, and we place ourselves in the hands of God for each trial.

7.   Protection from evil. When we ask for
       protection from evil we recognize that there is
       evil in the world and that we need God's
       continuous protection from it.

When we pray a prayer like this one, we should also
specifically mention things that are on our own
hearts. It is a prayer in which we lay everything on
the altar before God and place ourselves fully into his
caring hands.

Many prayers relate to a specific, urgent need that
occurs at a particular time--an *emergency*. But the
Lord's prayer refers to the constant state of your life
and to the constant relationship with God.

There are many prayer formulas, but if we would
acknowledge all these things and ask them of God
regularly, and put our trust in God and our minds on
Him, we would require far fewer *emergency* prayers.
Many of those prayers are simply pieces of this
larger prayer.

> You should praise the LORD for his love
> and for the wonderful things he does for all of
> us.
> To everyone who is thirsty, he gives something
> to drink;
> to everyone who is hungry,
> he gives good things to eat.
> (Psalm 107:8,9)

Using the Lord's Prayer as a Model

To use a scriptural prayer you take each point of the model and apply it to your situation. Sometimes there will be elements you can't use because they don't apply. Sometimes you will want to add things to the prayer. Occasionally one prayer might include things from various scriptural prayers and promises. Don't use written prayers to limit your prayer life. Use them as something to build on—something more personal.

The following table provides an example of the Lord's prayer turned into a *current* and *personal* prayer.

The Lord's Prayer	Notes	My Prayer
Our Father in heaven,	Address your Father in heaven. Here you can include anything that you want to say affirming the relationship with the Father.	Loving Father in heaven, I thank you for your love, your care, and your guidance to this point. I thank you for bringing me to the point of providing this example prayer.
help us to honor your name.	Pray to bring yourself into conformity with everything that brings honor to God.	Help me to give honor to your name as I write, speak and teach. Let me make everything that I do reflect honor and glory to you and you alone.
Come and set up your kingdom,	Bring God's kingdom into your life and into the world. Just because you may be the agent for accomplishing part of this	Set up your kingdom in my life, and let me spread that kingdom to those around me. Bring all earth under the sway of your

	doesn't mean you can't pray to God for it to happen. Also, remember to praise him afterward, even if you can identify the human agent. God works through human agents. Thank God and thank the human agent!	kingdom of love. Help me to obey you in the planning of my day.
so that everyone on earth will obey you, as you are obeyed in heaven.	Try to bring to mind a specific element of the kingdom and of obedience to the will of God. Ask for knowledge of his will.	You have said that everyone who loves knows God. What a place of love Heaven must be in your presence! Make us obedient to your law of love.
Give us our food for today.	God knows your needs, but you need to affirm them and affirm that God meets them. Again, remember to praise him for answered prayer.	Lord, I have physical needs for food and shelter. Supply my needs according to your will.

Forgive us for doing wrong,	The model prayer asks for forgiveness. God knows what you've done wrong, but do you? Part of confession and forgiveness is an acknowledgement of the problems.	Forgive me for my pride, for my critical attitude, for worrying when I know you can provide. Forgive me for failing to greet each person who needed a smile today. Forgive me for those I didn't notice. Help me to acknowledge them. Let me know where I have failed.
as we forgive others.	This is a hard part of the Lord's prayer. How many of us would really like to be forgiven in the way in which we forgive others? I think not many. Include in your prayer the request that you become so forgiving that you may pray this	Forgive me when I have been unforgiving! Make me so forgiving that I can sincerely ask you to forgive me as I forgive others. I forgive _____ for ignoring me today. I forgive _____ for telling someone else about my

	without a shudder; so that you can be happy to know that God will forgive you just as you forgive others. Ask God to give you more of his grace and mercy.	problem. Bless them, Lord, with more of Your presence. Draw closer to them and closer to me, Father.
Keep us from being tempted	Testing is going to happen, so why do we ask to be kept from temptation? I think that we ask so that we are reminded to stay away from it. Indeed we also ask for God's protection, but how many times do we ask God to protect us and then act like we want as much trouble as possible?	Lord, You know that there are temptations all around me, especially temptations to go right back to doing all the things I've just confessed. Guard me from my own tendencies to do evil. Prevent me from listening to the wrong voice and let me listen only to your voice.

| and protect us from evil. | | Cleanse me from the evil within, guard and protect me from the evil without.

In the name of your Son and in the understanding of the sacrifice made for me,

Amen |
| --- | --- | --- |

The prayer does not need to be longer than the model, but if you have many things to say under one category, such as the request for forgiveness, don't feel pressured to keep the prayer short. Don't feel pressured to make the prayer any particular length. The right length of a prayer is like the right length for your legs -- long enough to reach the ground!

Chapter 3 Questions and Exercises

1. Write your individual prayer following the pattern of the Lord's prayer. There is no right or wrong way to do this, but try to cover all the same elements, only use personal things from your own life.

2. When gathered in a group, write a group prayer that follows this same pattern. Have one person write the prayer down, while various members of the group provide petitions or praises that represent the feelings of the group.

3. Gather your group into a circle, and designate one member to pray the Lord's prayer phrase by phrase. After each phrase, the person who is reading the prayer should pause, and let people in the circle add short prayers that are brought to mind by that phrase. Again, there is no right or wrong way to do it, but the group will probably find it helpful to keep each individual statement or petition short, allowing everyone to say something each time if they want, and also allowing each person to say more than one thing after each phrase. Don't rush it!

4 - Simple Petitions

1. Identify your need
2. Seek the will of God
3. Submit to the will of God
4. Ask
5. Expect

Petition is the most basic form of prayer. You ask for what you need or want and you trust God to supply.

The promise on which this type of prayer is based is found in Matthew 7:7–"Ask, and you will receive. Search, and you will find. Knock, and the door will be opened for you."

There are many examples of petition model prayers in the Bible. The simplest of these is Luke 18:13–"God, have pity on me! I am such a sinner."

Keep it just that simple at the start.

Your petitions can take many forms. Sometimes you are simply asking—telling God what it is that you feel you need. Sometimes you will be crying out in distress, while at other times you will be claiming

God's promises for your daily needs. Whatever your situation, you can simply petition God.

In sermons, articles, and books on prayer you will find many different ways to pray. You will find many suggestions for the "right" way to approach God. Most of these are actually good suggestions, but they are not exclusive. You don't have to use any one of them, and when you are in need you don't need to worry about how you approach God.

Just talk.

Pull up a couple of chairs if that helps to make it more personal.

That's the key—just expressing yourself. You can combine the petition with praise and worship. You can quote Bible verses and remind God (and more importantly yourself) of his promises. But what God wants is to hear you express yourself to him from your heart. If all you can do is cry, do it! If you want to have a long conversation, do that! If you can only think of two or three words, that is just fine!

> Our prayers are the proper test of our desires; nothing being fit to have a place in our desires which is not fit to have a place in our prayers: what we may not pray for, neither should we desire. -- John Wesley

Chapter 4 Questions and Exercises

1. Are you comfortable asking God for things? Why or why not?

2. What might make you more comfortable bringing your requests to God?

Note: We do want to seek balance in our prayer life. Our prayer life should not consist solely of asking God for the things we need or want. But we should also not be afraid of asking. For now, concentrate on becoming comfortable with asking.

3. Get together in a group and tell one another what you would like to receive from the Lord. Be sure to include both physical and spiritual blessings.

4. Discuss in a group what your ideal life would be as a Christian. What would you like God to do for you? What would you like to do for God? Do you think this is possible? Is it in accordance with God's will for you? (It is very important that everyone in the group be courteous and respectful of the hopes and dreams of others in such a discussion. Don't put anyone down because their desires are too great or too small.)

22

5 - Intercessory Prayer

Intercessory prayer is simply prayer for other people. "If you have sinned, you should tell each other what you have done. Then you can pray for one another and be healed. *The prayer of an innocent person is powerful, and it can help a lot."* (James 5:16) In this sense everyone is called to be an intercessor as we pray for one another.

Intercessors: Read Colossians 1

There is a further level of intercessory prayer in which God lays a particular burden on certain people to pray. For example, you might feel a special call to pray for your city, your president, your pastor and family, or a friend. It is not how well <u>you</u> know the person or circumstance but how well <u>God</u> knows them.

In writing to the Colossian church, Paul speaks of continuing the suffering of Christ. After telling the Colossians that he has not stopped praying for them (Colossians 1:9), he continues to urge them to be deeply rooted and firm (verse 23) in the faith. Paul has an intercessory burden on behalf of the Colossian church.

If everyone is called to some form of intercessory prayer, why do we call some people "intercessors?" An intercessor is someone who is especially called and equipped by God through the Holy Spirit to spend time in earnest prayer for others. You become an intercessor simply by receiving such burdens from God to pray for others. You learn from the Holy Spirit how to pray for certain people or groups. "Ask me, and I will tell you things that you don't know and can't find out." (Jeremiah 33:3)

At many times in history God has searched for certain righteous people during times of judgment. In the time of Noah, only one family was found (Genesis 7:1). In Sodom, only Lot and his family were found. In Jerusalem God searched for anyone who was "truly upset and sad about the disgusting things" being done (Ezekiel 9:4).

And I sought for anyone among them who would repair the wall and stand in the breach before me on behalf of the land, so that I would not destroy it; but I found no one.
— Ezekiel 22:30 (NRSV)

Intercession is one of the gifts God has given to strengthen the body. Intercessors work under the authority of their pastor and church leaders just as anyone else in the church does.

Intercessors:
Review
1 Corinthians 11-14
Titus 2
Ephesians 4

Intercessors must be **listeners**. Intercessory prayer is prayer guided by the Spirit. We are not on our own in prayer; we have the Holy Spirit to guide us. Paul tells us in Romans that we do not know how to pray so the Holy Spirit helps us beyond what mere words can convey (Romans 8:26).

"Good Defense Makes a Strong Offense"

Many, **many** times an intercessor may find they are feeling tired and worn out. Temptation becomes more difficult to resist and discouragement becomes a daily companion. We may be 'suffering' with 'worldly sorrow'. How can you tell the difference between 'Godly sorrow' and 'worldly sorrow'?

"Now I rejoice, not because you were grieved, but because your grief led to repentance; for you felt a godly grief, so that you were not harmed in any way by us. For godly grief produces a repentance that leads to salvation and brings no regret, but worldly grief produces death." — 2 Corinthians 7:9, 10 (NRSV)

Some of the signs of worldly sorrow are:

♦ Wailing and moaning without looking ahead or stepping toward the victory that God has promised
♦ Absence of repentance where repentance is needed

- Depression
- A critical spirit toward those for whom you are praying
- Discouragement
- Losing your sense of God's presence
- Lack of fruit

You can have joy even in intercession because you are in a victorious army. You can see the fruits of your prayers by faith even through the gloom. "Faith makes us sure of what we hope for and gives us proof of what we cannot see." (Hebrews 11:1) We can see the light even from the deepest suffering: "Out of his anguish he shall see light; he shall find satisfaction through his knowledge." — Isaiah 53:11a (NRSV) A good guideline for intercessors is that they spend three times as much time in praise and worship as in intercession.

There are some simple, Biblical principles used by many heroes of the faith that will help to overcome this problem. We do **not** have to live in defeat! (Psalm 46) But first remember:

Every child of God can defeat the world, and our faith is what gives us this factory. – 1 John 5:4

- **Get some rest** Even Jesus took time off to rest (Mark 6:31).
- **Meet with other Christians** The writer of Hebrews reminds us of the importance of meeting

(Hebrews 10:25). It is a time of encouragement! Be sure that you include both giving and receiving encouragement. Don't be too proud to admit that you need it!

♦ **Praise God and worship Him** Praise and worship strengthens you and reminds you that the glory belongs to God. It reminds you that the battle doesn't depend on you and that you are not alone. Praise and worship is Scripture, prayer, music, dance,

Praise Scriptures:
Psalm 33
Psalm 104
Psalm 136
Psalm 149
Psalm 150
Isaiah 35
Isaiah 54

etc. Even if you can't sing or dance well, do it any way. It is not the style; it is the attitude of praise.

♦ **Confess, repent, renouce, then rejoice in God's forgiveness and cleansing.** There is no better expression of the benefit of forgiveness than: *Before I confessed my sins, my bones felt limp, and I groaned all day long. Night and day your hand weighed heavily on me, and my strength was gone as in the summer heat. So I confessed my sins and told them all to you. I said, "I'll tell the LORD each one of my sins." Then you forgave me and took away my guilt* (Psalm 32:3-5). When you have confessed your sins, claim your forgiveness and let God take those sins **away**!

♦ **Let others pray for you** Often prayer warriors assume that because they are praying and seeing the effects in other people's lives they don't need to receive prayer themselves. This is a prideful attitude. It is also a failing attitude!

Too much pride will destroy you. — Proverbs 16:18

Jesus said, "Simon, listen to me! Satan has demanded the right to test each one of you, as a farmer does when he separates wheat from the husks. But Simon, I have prayed that your faith will be strong. And when you have come back to me, help the others." — Luke 22:31, 32

♦ We should realize that we will be tested, that we need prayer to sustain us in the test, and that we need to then support our fellow Christians in their time of testing. ***Everyone*** will be in testing at some time and ***everyone*** will be supporting others at some time.

Chapter 5 Questions and Exercises

1. Look at the exercises for chapter 4 and try to imagine the same thing for a time when you pray for someone else. What would you want to ask God to do in their life? Don't be afraid to be open. Avoid "Sunday School" answers—talk about what you'd really like, not what you think you *should* like.

2. Where can you get information on people who need your prayers? Think of all the sources.

3. Consider keeping a prayer journal. This can be a simple notebook, with the date you begin praying, a short note about the prayer, and then leave space for answers. The key is that you know what has happened as you prayed for that person.

4. In a group, have each person make a list of the first three people who come to their mind for prayer. Then have each person share their list. Share the specifics **only** if it can properly be done in a group. *If you have information that is personal, no matter how you received it, don't share it without permission.* Look at the differences and similarities in the lists. Look at how many people are represented on those lists. Discuss how each of you might be praying for those people.

Chapter 5 Questions and Exercises

1. Look at the exercises on page 29.
Is your life a lot like this? Does it remind you of
someone else. What would you need to do to get
it to be like it should be to be from A to F...
Sunday School answers speak about what your
life is like, not what you think you should live.

2. Where can you get... foundation in your... who
need you... pray... how... that someone...

3. Consider... one... your journal... home... a
simple note... box with the date you began praying
about... about the... you've said... pray every...
... in... The... that you know... where... get...
happen... if you... pray... than... house...

4. ... pray... pray every... life of... the other
believers around... not only... briefly... pray
pray and... have... (Matthew...

... over the... those... who...
... of people...
small note... file... box... may... a...
report... most new... have... how to...
... right can... pray for those... our...

30

6 - Healing and Prayer

[Jesus said,] *"Father, it is time for you to glorify your son so that I may glorify you."*　　　　*John 17:1 (Jody Neufeld's paraphrase)*

The diseased state is not a natural one for the human body. When God completed His creation of people, he pronounced the work very good (Genesis 1:31). Disease is often viewed in scripture as a punishment (Exodus 15:26), but Jesus indicated that often it was not (John 9:1-5).

The church is the body of Christ (1 Corinthians 12:12, 13). We show Jesus to the world (1 John 1:1-3). Jesus constantly reached out to heal those in need. If the church wants to follow his example we must be a community of healing. We must reach out to provide both spiritual and physical healing, and to sustain those who are healed.

There are a number of ways to pray for someone for their healing:

◆ The elders of the church, or church leaders, may anoint a person with oil, and pray for their healing.

If you are sick, ask the church leaders to come and pray for you. Ask them to put olive oil on you in the name of the Lord. If you have faith when you pray for sick people, they will get well. The Lord will heal them, and if they have sinned, he will forgive them.
– James 5:14, 15

♦ Some people are given the gift of healing, so that they can lay hands on the sick, or simply command the disease to depart in the name of Jesus (1 Corinthians 12:9). (We should always remember that the authority is in the name of Jesus, and is not our own.)

Anyone can and should pray for those who are sick and suffering. We may wish to pray in different ways as the Spirit directs each one. Remember that it is not volume, wording, or some set of magical actions, but rather the power of God that heals people.

Very often in our prayers for physical healing, the amount of the person's faith or the amount of **my** faith as an intercessor is called into question. Yes, we **are** to have faith but the command to have faith means more than simply believing that what you do will work. It means:

✓ To place your trust in God and in His will and not in yourself, your power, or your will.

✓ To see beyond what can be noticed in the physical realm. "Faith makes us sure of what we hope for and gives us proof of what we cannot see." (Hebrews 11:1)

God desires that the person who is healed physically also be brought into a good relationship with Him. Jesus often indicated that the person who was receiving healing had been healed because of their faith. But He also spoke healing upon those who did not know Him nor exhibit great faith in the power of God (Matthew 9:18-26; John 11:1-44; Acts 9:36-43). It is good when praying for someone else's healing to pray also for God to increase our faith to receive healing.

Some people believe that if you seek medical treatment, you are denying God's power to heal. But God is the creator, the ultimate source of the knowledge which allows people to design remedies and procedures that will heal people. We should not reject one form of the power of God in order to depend on another. Rather, we should seek God's will in prayer, and make use of all that He provides to us for our healing.

The biggest question that we all must ponder when we look at prayer and healing is: Why isn't **everyone** healed?

But first we must answer the question: Why is *anyone* healed? We start our answer with God's promises of healing, but if we are to understand why healing occurs in some cases and not others, we may need to dig a little bit deeper.

In John 9 we have the story of Jesus healing a man born blind. As soon as the disciples saw this man their first question was, "Who sinned?" Bad things could only happen to people because of sins, and something bad had obviously happened to this man, so he must be a particularly gross sinner! But the disciples were wrong in a number of ways:

1. They were wrong in their focus: they were looking for some dirt they could discuss.
2. They were wrong in their concern: they were concerned over the theology, and not over the person.
3. They were wrong also in their mission: they were only interested in the immediate situation.

We most commonly fail on the third point, but we often do on the first two as well. Jesus shifted their focus and pointed them to the mission. "It wasn't that this man sinned or his parents; this happened so that God's glory could be revealed" (John 9:3).

When Jesus went on to heal the man, God's glory was revealed, and people came to discuss the mission of Jesus and what he had accomplished.

Jesus was concerned for the man himself, but he was also concerned for his broader mission.

We often try to look for someone to blame when a person is sick, and we look even more for someone to blame when many people pray for a person and that person is not healed. Someone possibly didn't have enough faith, they didn't pray enough, perhaps the person is cursed, or those who prayed did so in the wrong way.

But the bottom line is that we don't know why some people are healed and some are not. We just know that this has been the case throughout the history of the church. We know, in addition, that when we pray, some people are healed, and that is more than happens when we don't!

We also don't know God's total plan. While God does not normally cause particular diseases and suffering, God does make use of it for his glory. (God does cause suffering sometimes as discipline or as punishment. There are numerous instances of this in scripture.) We should look for the opportunities to glorify God that are provided by adversity.

One more point to consider is this: God is more concerned with your eternal state than he is with your physical condition. God wants you to do well and to be healthy, but he primarily asks you to accept the law of sowing and reaping. We must

combine faith and submission to God's will in our
prayers.

Chapter 6 Questions and Exercises

1. Look back at the exercises for chapter 5. Apply the exercises to people you know who have a specific need of physical or spiritual healing.

2. Share experiences of people for whom various group members have prayed for healing. Were these people physically healed? Discuss what else the Lord may have done in their lives even if there was not a physical healing or there was **more** than a physical healing.

3. "God answers our prayers better than we pray them." — Henry Neufeld. Does this bring a story to your mind where God answered differently and better than you asked?

7 - Repentance AND the Victory

Paul tells us that ALL are sinners and fall short of God's call to be holy. We do not **live** in His glory because we continue to sin.

Psalm 51 provides an example of repentance.

> I know about my sins, and I cannot forget my terrible guilt. v.3

1. **Acknowledge** – Completely admit to what you have done wrong, without excuses.

> Wash me with hyssop until I am clean and whiter than snow.   v.7

2. **Cleanse** – Ask God to cleanse you and make you whole.

> Make me as happy as you did when you saved me; make me want to obey!   v.12

3. **Restore** – Ask to be restored to God's favor.

> I will teach sinners your Law, and they will return to you. v.13

4. **Teach** -- You teach others by sharing your testimony about what God has done in your life.

> Help me to speak, and I will praise you, Lord.
> v.15

5. **Praise God** – Praise God for what He has done. This has the additional effect of reminding you of what He has done and keeping you humble before Him.

> Then you will be pleased with the proper sacrifices, and we will offer bulls on your altar once again.
> v.18, 19

6. **Worship** – Worship is the natural consequence of a relationship with God.

If you ask for forgiveness and still feel guilty, there are several ways in which repentance can fail.

♦ Making excuses instead of fully acknowledging guilt

See the story of Saul in 1 Samuel 15, especially verses 20 and 21. Instead of acknowledging his guilt, he denies it and adds an excuse. Let's look at the contrast between David's actions and Saul's actions:

40

David vs. Saul	
2 Samuel 11-12	1 Samuel 13-15
Murder and Adultery	Disobedience
Prophet sent	Prophet sent
Admits guilt	Denies guilt and makes excuses
Accepts punishment as just	Complains about punishment
Is accepted by God	Is rejected by God

♦ Not fully changing your mind about your actions.

To 'repent' means to 'change your mind'. If you are not determined to change, you have not really repented.

♦ No desire for cleansing

Forgiveness is followed by cleansing. If we don't want the cleansing, we won't receive the forgiveness.

♦ Refusing joy

Sometimes being sorrowful makes us feel important or even comforted, so we refuse the joy of restoration. Repentance puts us back in line with the heavenly attitude. Refusing joy takes us

back off the heavenly attitude. *"Jesus said, 'In the same way there is more happiness in heaven because of one sinner who turns to God than over ninety-nine good people who don't need to.'"*
— Luke 15:7

♦ Unworthiness

Feeling that you cannot possibly be cleansed or be fit for God's kingdom. But God has made us fit for his kingdom.

> All of this shows that God judges fairly and that he is making you fit to share in his kingdom for which you are suffering.

♦ Unbelief

Either you don't believe that God **can** forgive you or **will** forgive you. (See 1 John 1:9). Remember that our heavenly Father desires to give us good gifts.

> If you forgive others for the wrongs they do to you, your Father in heaven will forgive you. But if you don't forgive others, your Father will not forgive your sins. — Matthew 6:14, 15

♦ Unforgiveness

Unforgiveness includes holding onto our resentments and grudges. We can fail to forgive because we have been hurt to much. We can also fail to forgive because we refuse to admit that we have been hurt. [Jesus said,] *"You know that you have been taught, "An eye for an eye and a tooth for a tooth." But I tell you not to try to get even with a person who has done something to you."* — Matthew 5:38, 39a

There is a question that would be good to address at this time and that is: What is the 'unpardonable sin'?

Many people believe that the unpardonable sin is "grieving the Holy Spirit," but when asked what that means, they have a great deal more difficulty identifying the specific thing you might do in order to grieve the Holy Spirit.

Let me suggest simply that "grieving the Holy Spirit" is acting in such a way as to close your spiritual ears so you won't hear what the Holy Spirit has to say. The Spirit is what brings conviction of sin. If you refuse to listen so many times, you will become unable to hear. You will then not seek pardon for your sins, and not seek new life and new power in order to continue to walk with God. Your sin will be unpardonable because you will not ask for pardon.

For more information, see *Hebrews: A Participatory Study Guide*, Lesson 7 (page 40) and Appendix C (page 115) which includes my personal testimony of how God led me to this conclusion.

If upon examination we still struggle with the 'rejoicing', it is wonderful to know that one of the rewards in my ongoing relationship with God is building a **trust** relationship with Him. When we **trust** God for the final result even when we cannot see it – we can have peace and joy even in trouble.

> We gladly suffer, because we know that suffering helps us to endure. And endurance builds character, which gives us a hope that will never disappoint us.
> — Romans 5:3-5

Chapter 7 Questions and Exercises

1. Can you think of a time when you knew you needed to repent for something specific, but you just couldn't bring yourself to do it? If you have repented, what finally got you to do it? What makes repentance hard to do?

2. If your group is comfortable doing so, share personal stories about repentance. Do not pressure anyone to participate, but make them as comfortable as possible to do so.

3. Are there things your small group or even your church may need to repent of *as a group*? Some examples might be your witness as a congregation to the community, your willingness to reach out to the unlovely, the way the church treats visitors, the way the church has treated pastors in the past (or present), and so forth.

8 - Praying the Scriptures

What a wonderful concept! What could be better than **praying** the very words of God? Take any Scripture, a promise or a blessing and put yourself or someone you know as the subject or focus of the passage.

Example: Psalm 139 for myself
Lord, you know me. You know when I am in my house. You know when I am at my office. You know what I am thinking and what I am going to say before I do! I thank you that you protect me in all ways. That is almost too unbelievable to know! Thank you, Lord!...(vv.1-6)

Example: Ephesians 3:14-21 for a friend
With the powerful grace of God in mind, I kneel before you, Father. You are the One from whom every family in heaven and on earth gets its name. All fame belongs to You. I ask, Father, that You give _____ the power to reach into the inner man by the Spirit. I ask that Christ will dwell in *his* understanding through faith. I ask that with all the saints *he* be rooted deeply and grounded firmly in love, and be able to grasp just how wide and long and high and deep Your love is. May *he* know it,

even though it is too great to really understand, so *he* may be filled with Your fullness. Father, I give You the glory. May You receive praise from generation to generation forever, because You are the One Who works among us so powerfully that You are able to do more than we can ask or even imagine.

Example: The Armor of God, Ephesians 6:10-17
Note: This is available as a book mark from Pacesetters Bible School, Inc.[1]

Father, in the name and authority of Jesus, I pray on the armor of God. The Helmet of Salvation — that I **know** with certainty that I am bought with a price and the child of a king. The Breastplate of Righteousness — not anything I can earn. It is a free gift. It is Jesus' righteousness, given to me. I can enter the Holy of Holies and be with You, Father. The Belt of Truth — seal it on me with the Blood of Jesus. I want to hear and know only Your voice. All others are deceivers. The Shoes of Peace — ready to take the Gospel into all the world. I speak peace into all my storms, all winds and waves – peace. The Shield of Faith — Father, increase my faith. Increase the shield above my head, below my feet, and around my body. Holy Spirit, be my rear guard. The Sword of the Spirit, the Word of God. Lord, increase my hunger for your Word. May it be nourishment to my spirit. Lord, wrap me in the cloak of humility. **ALL** glory, honor, and praise

---

[1] http://www.biblepacesetter.org

belong to You. I am **only** an ordinary instrument in the hands of an extra-ordinary God. Seal me in the Blood of Jesus. I charge warrior angels around me. I consecrate all that I steward to you, Lord. Use me this day as you will.   Amen.

Suggestion: Keep a prayer journal.   It can be something just as simple as a small note pad. Jot down the date, a note about the prayer, and leave room to record God's answer.

Chapter 8 Questions and Exercises

1. Choose your own scripture passage and pray it for someone you know. Use the examples in this chapter to help you. In addition you can find adapted prayer passages in our pamphlet *Prayer Scriptures for Prayer Warriors*[2] and in chapter 2 of this booklet.

2. As an individual exercise, choose a passage of scripture to read, and then as you find specific promises, commands, or incidents in that passage, pray those scriptures for a particular individual or group. A good procedure to follow is:

- ✓ Pray for the Holy Spirit's guidance
- ✓ Spend some time listening
- ✓ Choose a person or group that comes to your mind
- ✓ Choose a passage that comes to mind[3]
- ✓ Read slowly, spending time listening to the Holy Spirit
- ✓ Stop on a passage if you hear the Holy Spirit guiding you to do so

------

[2]http://participatorystudyseries.com/prayer_scriptures.shtml
[3] Check the list of scriptures in chapter 2, use a concordance, or find one of the many Bible promise books that are available. In addition, there is an index of prayer scriptures on our web site, http://energion.com/prayer.

If the passage is a command, you can pray for obedience, if it is a positive incident in someone's life, you can pray that someone will have the courage to behave that positively, you can pray that someone will avoid a negative incident. You can pray that one of God's promises will be fulfilled in their life.

The key is to listen for the guidance of the Holy Spirit.

(I first used this approach in praying for a group of college students. I prayed through the book of Ezekiel for them, and found the experience amazingly powerful. – Henry Neufeld)

9 - Getting Answers

The story of Jonah is a very interesting one in the
Bible. It is actually somewhat of a comedy. Read
Jonah first just to enjoy the humor in the situation!

When I speak to classes about the Jonah problem,
the temptation is for some to think that I'm going to
talk about the problem of running away from God.
Now running away from God is certainly a problem,
but not the one I have in mind. The problem I have
in mind is easily solved. When God speaks, listen!

Next, someone will always mention the problem of
the big miracle. How big a fish can God make, and
can he keep Jonah alive in the belly of whatever fish
he makes? But I'm not concerned with the weight of
fish. God can, and probably will, do what he wants
to.

No, the Jonah problem is a bit more difficult than
either of those. It starts with Jonah 4:1 — "Jonah
was really upset and angry." No, the Jonah problem
is not anger either!

Why was Jonah upset and angry? He had finally
fulfilled God's mission and preached to the Ninevites.
Under his preaching 120,000 people had turned to

the Lord and repented. What preacher could possibly be upset with that? It seems like an extraordinary miracle, of a proportion never witnessed elsewhere in the world.

The problem is in the message God sent and in the way Jonah saw that message.

How God and Jonah view Nineveh	
God	**Jonah**
Wants Ninevites to repent (change)	Wants the Ninevites to be what they have been
Loves the Ninevites	Hates the Ninevites
Wants to spare the Ninevites	Hopes they burn slowly
Loves the Ninevites enough to give his life	Hates the Ninevites enough to give his life
Is interested in the results of the message	Is concerned that people think he made an accurate prediction
Responds to the people's needs	Sticks to his own agenda

Jonah is waiting for God to act. What's wrong with that? Jonah is waiting for a miracle, but a miracle has already come. Because he is not watching for what God actually does, but only for what **he** wants God to do, he misses the miracle happening before his eyes as 120,000 people repent under his preaching. Jonah's agenda doesn't match God's agenda, so he misses the action that God is taking even while he is a part of it!

This is **the Jonah problem.**

Sometimes the Jonah problem is created by hatred.
We haven't learned to love the people God loves as
much as God loves them. And who has? But
sometimes we experience the Jonah problem just
because we have become certain of our own way and
too proud to listen to the voice of God whether sent
directly or through some of his servants. Open eyes,
open heart, and open mind are the protection
against this problem.

A prayer against the Jonah problem:

**Lord, give me wisdom liberally as you promised
in James 1:5. Help me to have my eyes opened
to what you are doing and how you are doing
it. Let me see you in action as Elisha's servant
did when you opened his eyes to your army
arrayed to protect him (2 Kings 6:8-22). Open
my eyes to see, my heart to love and my mind
to understand. In Jesus' name, Amen.**

Chapter 9 Questions and Exercises

Individually and in a group, think of experiences in your life when you might have thought your prayer was not answered. Don't be afraid to admit what you wanted God to do, and that this did not happen. Then consider those incidents from the perspective of the Jonah problem.

1. Are there any incidents in which God did something else that turned out to be better in the end?

2. Are there any incidents in which God was silent and that helped you to grow?

3. Are there any incidents in which you're pretty sure you asked for something you shouldn't have?

4. Are there any incidents in which you now think you were wrongly motivated? (For example, perhaps you prayed that something bad happen in someone else's life, or that you would get revenge.)

5. Are there any examples of incidents in which you still don't understand the result? (Don't be afraid to admit this. In fact, it's likely that many incidents will fall into this category.) Pray for understanding or resolution in those incidents.

"Is not this the kind of fasting I have chosen: to loose the chains of injustice and untie the cords of the yoke, to set the oppressed free and break every yoke? Is it not to share your food with the hungry and to provide the poor wanderer with shelter— when you see the naked, to clothe him, and not to turn away from your own flesh and blood?"
– Isaiah 58:6-7

10 - Fasting and Prayer

In the Bible fasting refers to restricting one's diet, including refraining from eating and drinking entirely. As Isaiah says (Isaiah 58:6-7), fasting can include other activities that are done for God.

In modern times, fasting has been extended to include giving up other activities that are part of one's routine, generally things that one enjoys.

Some types of fasts include not eating for one or more meals, not eating and drinking for a short period of time (always consider your health), leaving off certain types of entertainment (an evening with the TV turned off), and limiting your diet such as not eating sweets, or drinking soft drinks. These are only a few examples.

The Purpose of Fasting

Fasting is not a way of getting God's attention. You already have God's attention—God doesn't have any trouble keeping up with what people are doing. But fasting does have to do with helping us get closer to God, mostly by focusing our attention on God.

The fast that God chooses, as discussed in Isaiah 58, has to do with treating other people appropriately and carrying out God's mission. If we are not right with God, fasting is not going to persuade Him to do things He would not otherwise do.

What fasting can do is help us focus on God and bring ourselves more into harmony with what God wants us to do.

In a fast, when you think of the thing you have given up, it should be a reminder to focus your attention on God and to listen for God's will. Sometimes God's will might be for you to quit fasting, and take some form of action.

In prayer we tell God how we are feeling and thinking and what we want. Prayer, in the sense of speaking to God, should include time for listening to God's will. Fasting is especially useful in focusing us on God's will and on how we can come closer to God's plan for us. The primary impact of fasting is on our listening to what the Holy Spirit wants to communicate to us.

Fasting and Health

Do not fast if there is a question of health. If you want to find something to help you focus on God find something that you can leave off that does not threaten your health. Cooperate with your physician. If you have questions about the wisdom of fasting, consult your physician and also your pastor or someone who helps keep you accountable.

Examples of Types of Fasts

√ One or two meals.
This is the most common type of fast. Some people will fast a single meal in a day, or fast from the morning until some time in the afternoon or evening. This can be done either a single time, or regularly on a particular day of the week.
√ All food for a period of time, but continuing liquids.
Leaving off all food for a specific period of time. Be certain that your health is good enough for this type of fast. (Any food fast should be considered carefully.)
√ Limited food and drink.
Again, this fast is done for a period of time. Ezekiel went on an extended fast of this type. If we understand the measures correctly, however, Ezekiel was miraculously sustained through his fast.
√ All food and drink for a period of time.
While this kind of fast, usually for a day or so, can be very useful, it is also the most dangerous, because the human body does not function well without water for very long.
√ Limiting entertainment or reading
Limiting movies, television viewing, or the type of books that one reads can help focus your mind on spiritual things.

The key to the best type of fast for you is to discover what helps you focus on God. That is the best fast for you.

Chapter 10 Questions and Exercises

1. What do you think about fasting? Does it make you feel good? Do you feel that someone who is fasting is self-righteous? Why?

2. If your health will allow it, choose a particular fast to carry out during the next week. If you are not in the habit of fasting, choose something simple. Share your experiences with a group later if possible. If your health will not allow fasting from food, consider one of the options listed under exercise 3.

3. List some things you could give up for a period of time. Some examples might be television, secular reading, or certain types of music. Consider something that will help you spend more time with God. Determine a period of time and "fast" from that activity, using the time you have freed up to spend time with God. Some people find this form of fasting more effective than fasting from food.

11 - Praying with Others

Praying with other people is a topic of its own. You may want to look at our companion volume, *When 3 to 8 Gather*, which deals with prayer groups. But for this introduction to prayer here are some basic ideas about praying with and for other people.

Sensitivity

Praying with others requires sensitivity. This involves listening to others and being sensitive to their wants and needs. Prayer is very personal. You communicate with God in the ways that work best in your relationship with God. But when you start praying with others you need to work together so you can build up and encourage one another as well as communicate your requests to God.

Here's a basic rule for praying or worshipping together: ***Do only the things that you can all agree on and participate in.***

This doesn't mean that you have to give up your own way of praying and worshipping, but simply that when you are together you do the things you can unite on. In particular circumstances, you might agree to try ideas in prayer and worship that one or another member of the group is not acquainted with, but you need to do that with sensitivity and be sure that the unity of the group is not hindered.

One on One Prayer

The simplest form of praying with others is praying one on one for someone else. Your method of prayer can be anything you are comfortable with. Simply follow these steps:

- √ Make yourself available without pressure
  Let the other person know you are willing to pray.
- √ Keep it simple
  If someone has shared a problem with you, just pray about that. Listen to the Holy Spirit for anything else, but also be open to the command to stop.
- √ Pray now
  If someone is comfortable having you pray with them, don't delay it. If they are uncomfortable find a time on your own to pray for them.
- √ Follow up if possible
  Don't just pray and forget about the person. You may not be able to follow up, but if you can, ask that person how they are doing.

Prayer Groups

Praying with groups is again simply a matter of being sensitive to others. Two or more people can meet at any time to pray together.

Remember:

√ Find a group that is united in their need for prayer and fellowship
√ Meet regularly
√ Be sensitive to the needs of all group members

Jesus said:

"For where two or three are gathered in my name, I am there among them." – Matthew 18:20

Chapter 11 – Questions and Exercises

1. Are you part of a prayer group? Why or why not?

2. If someone approaches at church and says they have a need and would like prayer, which of the following do you do?

     a. Promise to pray for them
     b. Give a non-committal response
     c. Pray for them right there
     d. Put them on the church prayer list
     e. Other response

Discuss why you would respond as you said you would. Do you think you should change your response? Why?

12 - Conclusion: Do It!

You probably picked this book up because you were interested in praying. That means God has been talking to you and calling you to pray. He wants to talk with you.

Begin to pray now! Don't wait! God is ready to listen.

If you spend money for the gym or for food so that your physical body remains healthy, how much more show you do to maintain your spiritual health.

It's not complicated.

Just do it!

Scripture Index

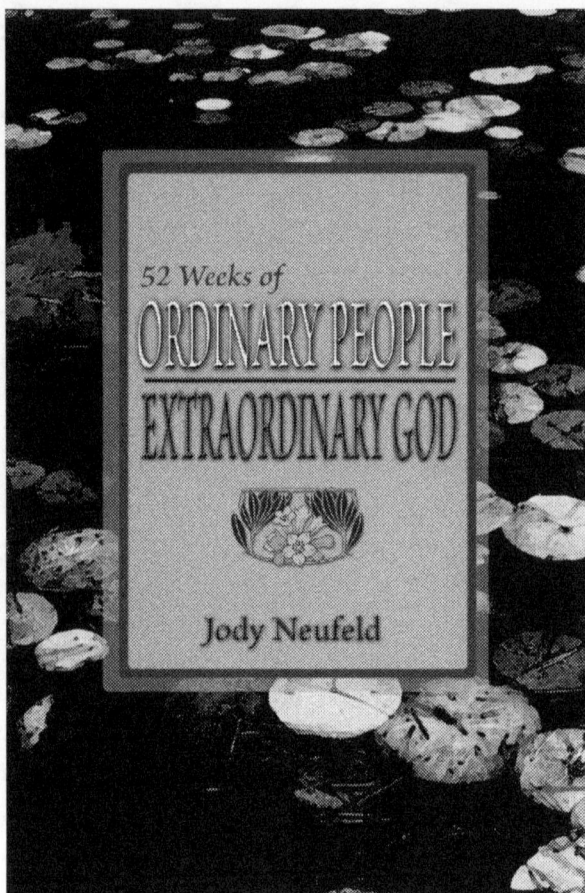

Ideal for prayer and study groups!

Jody Neufeld's daily devotional book, Daily Devotions of Ordinary People – Extraordinary God has become a favorite of many for individual devotional reading. This small, weekly book has 52 devotions along with study and discussion questions for small groups that meet weekly. Call us at (805) 968-1001 or see our web site (http://www.energionpubs.com) for quantity discounts. Suggested Retail: $7.99.

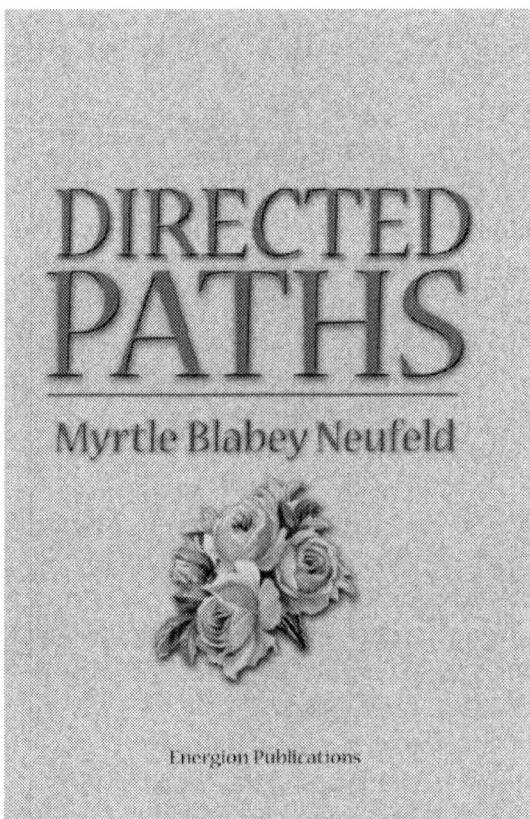

Strengthen your prayer life through testimony!

Retired missionary nurse Myrtle Blabey Neufeld tells stories of answered prayer in her life. These stories will strengthen your faith and encourage you to go further with God. One reader said, "Every story has a scripture and a lesson. I love it!" Another said, "Just wanted to tell you how much I enjoyed the book written by Mrs. Neufeld. What a gem she is!! I couldn't put it down until it was finished." Suggested Retail: $7.99. See our web site (http://www.energionpubs.com) or call (850) 968-1001.

Participatory Study Series Pamphlets

Energion Publications publishes a number of pamphlets on prayer and other topics important for Christians. These can be used in outreach and in Christian education programs. They are especially useful as handouts, and cover many of the topics contained in this booklet (*I Want to Pray!*).

Some titles are:

- ✓ I Want to Pray! (Pamphlet)
  Prayer basics
- ✓ Prayer Scriptures for Prayer Warriors
  Adapted scriptures for use in prayer. Learn to use the scriptures effectively in prayer.
- ✓ Self Defense for Prayer Warriors
  How to stay healthy spiritually while being in prayer for others.
- ✓ So You're an Intercessor
  What is intercession and who does it?
- ✓ Seven Barriers to Hearing the Word
  How can you remove the barriers that keep you from hearing from God?
- ✓ I Want to be Healed!
  Healing prayer, its effectiveness, and how to deal with apparent failure.

All pamphlets are available in PDF and Microsoft Word format and can be downloaded and printed in any quantity desired. You can also order them from us preprinted if you prefer not to print them yourself. Check out these resources at;

http://www.participatorystudyseries.com

www.ingramcontent.com/pod-product-compliance
Lightning Source LLC
Chambersburg PA
CBHW031606040426
42452CB00006B/429